EXHIBITION GUIDE

Monet Renoir and the Impressionist Landscape

EXHIBITION GUIDE

Monet
Renoir and the
Impressionist
Landscape

NATIONAL GALLERY OF IRELAND / MUSEUM OF FINE ARTS, BOSTON

This exhibition guide was published by the National Gallery of Ireland, Dublin, on the occasion of the exhibition

Monet, Renoir and the Impressionist Landscape

at the National Gallery of Ireland,
Millennium Wing, Clare Street, Dublin 2
22 January – 14 April 2002

This exhibition catalogue was produced with the support of the Department of Arts, Heritage, Gaeltacht and the Islands, and Eagle Star.

An Roinn Ealaíon, Oidhreachta,
Gaeltachta agus Oileán
Department of Arts, Heritage,
Gaeltacht and the Islands

ISBN 0903162970

Co-ordinated by Fionnuala Croke
Edited by Elizabeth Mayes
Designed by David Hayes
Printed and bound by Snoeck-Ducaju & Zoon, Belgium

Front cover: detail of Claude Monet, *Camille Monet and a Child in the Artist's Garden in Argenteuil*, 1875, Museum of Fine Arts, Boston. Anonymous Gift in Memory of Mr. and Mrs. Edwin S. Webster (1976.833)

Contents

EAGLE STAR

Eagle star is delighted to be associated with the *Monet, Renoir and the Impressionist Landscape* Exhibition and I would like to congratulate the National Gallery of Ireland on bringing this prestigious exhibition from the Museum of Fine Arts, in Boston, to Ireland and Dublin, the only European venue for the exhibition.

The first years of a new century are a good time to look back as well as forward, and the paintings included in Monet, Renoir and the Impressionist Landscape have found almost universal appeal over the last hundred years and will surely provide inspiration well into the new millennium.

The timing of the exhibition is of great significance as The National Gallery of Ireland celebrates the opening of the Millennium Wing. This is one of the most interesting new buildings in Dublin and it brings the opportunity to view wonderful masterpieces in a purpose-built environment.

Eagle Star as an Irish company, and a member of the international Zurich Financial Services Group, believes that our support of the National Gallery of Ireland fits well with our broader commitment to good Corporate Citizenship in all its aspects.

Michael Brennan
Managing Director

The Millennium Wing at the National Gallery of Ireland

RAYMOND KEAVENEY
DIRECTOR
THE NATIONAL GALLERY OF IRELAND

LIKE MANY OF THE MOST distinguished art institutions around the world, including the Victoria and Albert Museum, London (following the Crystal Palace Exhibition of 1851), Philadelphia Museum of Art (following the city's centennial exhibition of 1876) and the Musée du Petit Palais, Paris (following the Exposition Universelle of 1900), the National Gallery of Ireland was established as a direct response to one of the great nineteenth-century exhibitions. These mammoth events had their modest origins in France in the late eighteenth century before gathering momentum to become engines of industrial and cultural growth by the mid-1800s. While in most instances the exhibitions were focused on trade and industry, there was usually a strong cultural content which invariably proved immensely popular with the public. This popularity persuaded many governments and municipalities to promote the provision of more permanent accommodation for the display of art, both for the education of young artists and for the enjoyment of the general public.

In Ireland the catalyst for such an outcome was the Irish Industrial Exhibition of 1853 which was held in the grounds of Leinster House, then the property of the Royal Dublin Society. Such was the enormous popular success of this project, that a committee was formed to honour William Dargan, who had underwritten the cost of the event. The Dargan Memorial Committee joined forces with the newly established Irish Institution, which had come together in the wake of the exhibition with a view to establishing a National Gallery of Art. By August 1854 they had achieved their goal with the passing in Parliament of the Bill 'to provide for the Establishment of a National Gallery of Paintings, Sculpture, and the Fine Arts'.

The new, purpose-built Gallery, designed by the Tyrone-born architect, Francis Fowke, opened in January 1864. Since that date it has been enlarged three times by the construction of additional wings, each roughly comparable in size to the original building which faces onto Merrion Square. The first extension was completed in 1903, the second in 1968 and the most recent in January 2002, the latter opening up a new front onto the busy thoroughfare at Clare Street, opposite Trinity College.

While the first two extensions were designed primarily to accommodate the growth of the collection, which has risen from some 125 to approximately 2,500 paintings (not counting a collection of approximately 8,500 works on paper and around 350 works of sculpture), the most recent addition, the Millennium Wing, has particularly taken into account the need for improved facilities for the hosting of exhibitions. The management of exhibitions in recent times was facilitated, in the first instance, by the construction of the 1968 extension (Beit Wing), which, though not specifically designed to host temporary events, at least provided the Gallery with substantial additional accommodation and the scope to mount shows within the complex of buildings on Merrion Square. From the late 1960s to the present day numerous exhibitions were organised, mostly devoted to Irish art, although there were, from time to time, presentations of old master paintings and drawings from abroad. A notable aspect of many of these temporary presentations was the itinerant nature of the event, as a variety of rooms within the Gallery complex had to be found in which to mount the exhibits, there being no formally approved exhibition space. A regrettable consequence of this circumstance was the requirement to take down large sections of the permanent collection from display to accommodate each exhibition.

The benefits of managing a vigorous exhibitions programme were generally acknowledged and in the late 1980s consideration was given to the provision of a dedicated space in which to present temporary shows, a space which would not only allow the Gallery to continue to mount major events devoted to Irish art, but also to attract exhibitions from abroad, confident in the knowledge that it was equipped to the highest international standards. In this respect it can be noted that the Gallery has traditionally lent to major shows abroad – always on the understanding that the organising museum could guarantee appropriate conditions for the loan. Indeed, as part of the initiative to support the funding of the new Millennium Wing, the Gallery toured a number of complete shows from its collection to Australia, Japan and the United States.

The opportunity to acquire a site for a new wing presented itself towards the end of the 1980s when a property directly adjacent to the Gallery became available for purchase. Some five years after the acquisition of the property, and following the guarantee from Government of funding from the European Community, European Regional Development Fund, together with the generosity of numerous corporate and individual benefactors, the Gallery set about determining the brief for an international competition to select an architect to design the new building. Central to the design brief was the provision of purpose-built accommodation to host exhibitions, including new display galleries, customised art handling facilities, tight environmental controls, and an exhibition environment which enjoyed the benefit of controlled, natural light. In addition to the care of the exhibits, considerable attention was given to the comfort of visitors, including the provision of expanded dining and retail facilities, as well as generous, clearly laid out circulation spaces which link seamlessly with the existing buildings where the permanent collection, with its superb array of Irish and old master paintings, remains on view. Following the appointment of the firm of Benson and Forsyth as architects in 1996, work began on the project in 1999 and the completed building, replete with two main suites of galleries arranged over two levels, was ready for inauguration in January 2002.

As a piece of civic architecture, the new building makes a substantial contribution to the contemporary cityscape of Dublin, where its demonstrably modern facade sits comfortably among its elegant Georgian neighbours. The street elevation, in Portland stone and glass, makes a bold, yet essentially mannerly, statement which manages to remain in harmony with the fabric of the city which, for the most part, is constructed in brick and stone. The new building, unlike its Victorian counterpart on Merrion Square, stands directly on the main thoroughfare, giving the Gallery a very real and vital presence in the public perception. While the original entrance on the Square will continue to be used, most visitors will find the new entrance on Clare Street more convenient, as it is more accessible from public transport and closer to the main shopping precinct. The entrance lobby is tall and spacious and directly adjacent to the main Gallery shop and dining areas, with stairs and lifts giving direct access to the exhibition galleries.

A key decision in preparing for the opening of the Millennium Wing was to determine which paintings would go on display in the lower suite of galleries, a section of the new building which would normally be reserved for displaying works from the permanent

The National Gallery of Ireland, Main Entrance, Merrion Square West, Dublin.

collection. Given that the Irish collection numbers some 1,500 works, it was decided that this space would initially house Irish art of the first half of the twentieth century. It was then left to determine what would be the first exhibition to be hosted in the new suite of galleries located on the upper level. After much deliberation, it was agreed to present an exhibition focusing on the landscape painting of the French Impressionists. Given the enormous success of the Irish Impressionists exhibition some fifteen years earlier (1984), the presentation of the French Impressionists would surely enjoy popular support and provide the Irish public with a unique opportunity to view and enjoy the work of this generation of artists whose works attract large audiences whenever they are exhibited around the world.

Apart from its purely popular appeal, this very special exhibition has many resonances with the existing holdings of the National Gallery of Ireland, though it must sadly be acknowledged that within the collection itself, the representation of the French Impressionists is modest. It could have been very different. At a time when this small group of artists was changing the history of European art, the true nature of their vision was little appreciated in their native country and it was left to foreigners, most ostensibly to American collectors, to sustain their economic viability. It was this phenomenon which led to the enrichment of many American collections in holdings of Impressionist paintings, of which the Museum of Fine Arts in Boston is among the most outstanding.

It was was not only in America, however, that the new generation of artists found an appreciative audience. One of their most enthusiastic admirers was Sir Hugh Lane, a former Director of the National Gallery of Ireland, who, in the course of his tragically short life, assembled a remarkable collection of Impressionist art, including works by Degas, Manet, Monet and Renoir. However, while Lane bequeathed some of his most treasured paintings to the National Gallery of Ireland after his death in 1915, his Impressionist paintings were not among them, as he considered such works more appropriate to a gallery of modern art. To this end he aspired to the establishment of a gallery of modern art in Dublin and engaged the services of Sir Edwin Luytens to design a suitable building. The proposed gallery, which was to span the river Liffey, never materialised and the consequent fallout constitutes one of the great controversies in the history of Irish cultural life. Lane's thirty-nine modern paintings were lost to London, where they remained until 1959, when agreement was reached to share the works between London and Dublin. The present exhibition allows us to reassess the extent of this lost opportunity, which, for generations, stalled the collection of the work of these extraordinary artists, and, to the detriment of their public, limited the vision of our public institutions.

We are immensely grateful to the Board of Trustees of the Museum of Fine Arts in Boston for agreeing to make this marvellous exhibition available to us as the inaugural event for our Millennium Wing. In managing all the complex details of the preparations, we are hugely indebted to the Director, Malcolm Rogers, and his colleagues for all their expert support. We would also like to acknowledge the support of Minister Síle de Valera and the Department of Arts, Heritage, Gaeltacht and the Islands in bringing this prestigious exhibition to the National Gallery of Ireland.

Monet, Renoir and the Impressionist Landscape

GEORGE T.M. SHACKELFORD
CHAIR, ART OF EUROPE,
MUSEUM OF FINE ARTS, BOSTON

Monet, renoir and the impressionist landscape presents a selection of sixty-nine paintings by Claude Monet, Pierre-Auguste Renoir, and their contemporaries, as well as by painters of the generation before and after them who inspired the Impressionists or who were inspired by them. This exhibition is a rich survey of French landscape painting from the time of its great rise to prominence in the 1850s through the end of the nineteenth century. It begins with the roots of the Impressionist landscape in the art of Camille Corot and the Barbizon School and extends as far as the Post-Impressionist landscapes of Paul Gauguin and Vincent van Gogh.

The exhibition is drawn entirely from the great collection of paintings at the Museum of Fine Arts, Boston, and showcases some of its most famous Impressionist works: Monet's *Grainstack (Sunset)* (cat. no. 49)[1], Renoir's *Rocky Crags at L'Estaque* (cat. no. 57), Degas's *At the Races in the Countryside* (cat. no. 32), Cézanne's *Turn in the Road* (cat. no. 35), and van Gogh's *Houses at Auvers* (cat. no. 66). But the exhibition also features astonishing works, newly brought to light from Boston's collection, by artists whose fame in the late twentieth century has been overshadowed by that of the Impressionist generation: Paul Huet's *Landscape in the South of France* (cat. no. 4), Théodore Rousseau's *Gathering Wood in the Forest of Fontainebleau* (cat. no. 10), and Antoine Chintreuil's *Peasants in a Field* (cat. no. 11), to name a few.

Edgar Degas,
At the Races in the Countryside (detail).

The story of the Impressionist landscape and its development is complex, yet too often it has been reduced to a simple and direct trajectory: from the *plein-air* cloud studies of John Constable to the freely painted compositions of the Barbizon school; from Monet's *Impression: Sunrise* to the sunstruck landscapes of van Gogh at Arles, Saint-Rémy, and Auvers. This story recognises the fact that the Impressionists rejected the fussy, overly finished effects of paintings intended for exhibition at the official Salons and that they opted instead to paint sketchlike compositions in the open air and to exhibit these 'impressions' as finished works, forging a modern landscape style, much to the consternation of critics and the public.

It is a story that is undoubtedly true, but it tells only one of the many ways in which the art of landscape emerged from the achievements of the 'Men of 1830', as Corot and his contemporaries were called; and its development in the 1860s, 1870s, and 1880s was not a simple linear progression away from the preoccupations of an official style and toward a modernist idiom. This exhibition attempts to trace some of the major paths

5

of that development. Including not only the works of the indisputably Impressionist landscape painters – Monet and Renoir, with Cézanne, Degas, Pissarro, and Sisley – but also of their more traditionalist contemporaries – François-Louis Français and Henri-Joseph Harpignies, for example – the exhibition seeks to enrich the story of the Impressionist landscape by pointing out interesting byways that intersect or branch off from those pathways over time.

The story of the Impressionist landscape is intimately tied to the career of Claude Monet, its most famous, most steadfast, and arguably most innovative practitioner. In 1857, when Monet was sixteen, he met the marine painter Eugène Boudin, who took an interest in the young man and invited him along to paint in the open air. Later, Monet said that the experience was revelatory for him: 'Boudin, with untiring kindness, undertook my education. My eyes were finally opened and I really understood nature; I learned at the same time to love it.'[2] Boudin became Monet's unofficial teacher for several years, and his gift for painting skies was matched by the talents of the younger artist.

In May 1859 Monet went to Paris to see the Salon exhibition, which had opened on 15 April, and to try his hand at learning more about painting landscape. In that year, writing to Boudin from the capital, Monet singled out for praise the landscapes he saw at the Salon by Constant Troyon, Charles-François Daubigny, Théodore Rousseau, and Camille Corot. Troyon's paintings – *Return to the Farm* and *View Taken from the Heights of Suresnes* (Musée d'Orsay and Musée du Louvre, Paris) – were particularly attractive to Monet, who admired the older artist's ability to capture the fleeting effects of clouds, sunlight, and atmosphere. 'A magnificent sky,' he wrote, 'a stormy sky. There is a lot of movement, of wind in these clouds.'[3] Earlier, Monet had visited Troyon in his studio, and he immediately recognized Troyon's skill. 'I could not begin to describe all the lovely things I saw there,' he wrote to Boudin. Looking at Monet's canvases, Troyon advised the young man to learn how to draw by studying the human figure, at that time the foundation of every artist's education. 'Don't neglect painting,' he nevertheless told Monet, 'go to the country from time to time and make studies, and above all develop them.'[4] Monet might well have seen in Troyon's studio the kind of sketches made in the open air, such as *Fields outside Paris* (cat. no. 7), which Troyon would then develop and refine into easel paintings for the Paris art market – for example, *Sheep and Shepherd in a Landscape* (cat. no. 8) – and which also lay behind the large-scale pictures he painted for the official Salon exhibitions.

In the Salon, still controlled by the Academy, as well as in the more informal market of picture dealers, landscape had taken the place of history painting in the public imagination and in the minds and hearts of critics. Monet, recognising the hegemony of landscape painting, was determined to follow the path on which he had set out under Boudin. Still, taking Troyon's advice, in 1860 he embarked on a course of study to learn to draw the human figure, entering an informal art school – the Académie Suisse. In 1862 he entered the studio of Charles Gleyre, a history painter, where he met Pierre-Auguste Renoir, James McNeill Whistler, and Frédéric Bazille, each of whom practised not only figure painting but also landscape, and Alfred Sisley, who was to devote himself to pure landscape. In addition to his study from the model, Monet continued to paint landscape during excursions to the countryside near Paris, notably at the village of Chailly, near Barbizon, in the Forest of Fontainebleau.

The most important painters of the landscape vanguard had practised their craft in this region since the 1840s, among them Corot, Rousseau, Troyon, Narcisse-Virgile Diaz de la Peña, Jean-François Millet, and Gustave Courbet. In the years before and after the Revolution of 1848, the rise of Realism in French painting had given forth not only the heroic figural compositions of Millet and Courbet, but also a new notion of how landscape should be interpreted. Painters such as Corot or Rousseau sought to depict commonplace sites – ordinary meadows, fields, or woodlands – and to invest these simple landscapes with both a sense of poetry and a sense of the quiet dignity of the earth itself.

Aware of the special associations of the Fontainebleau landscape, Monet spent much of the spring of 1863 in Chailly and he returned in the following year. At this period in his development, the majority of Monet's subjects and compositions reflected his awareness of the art of these masters, as well as the continuing importance of Boudin and Johan Barthold Jongkind, a Dutch marine painter whom Monet had met on the Normandy coast in 1862 (see cat. nos. 20 and 21).

Boudin's influence on Monet, however strong, was by no means exclusive, even in the early 1860s. Although Boudin's masterly views of Normandy's ports and beaches (see cat. nos. 22–26) depicted light in the fractured manner that Monet was to perfect later in his career, Monet was also influenced by the boldly painted landscapes of Gustave Courbet, whose *Stream in the Forest* (cat. no. 17) was painted about 1862. Courbet's earthy palette and his preference for dense, boldly painted canvases may have inspired Monet again when, about 1864, he took his easel into the streets of Honfleur, near Le Havre, to paint on site a view of the Rue de la Bavolle (cat. no. 39).[5] Perhaps following Troyon's advice to 'develop' his studies, Monet used this *plein-air* canvas as the basis for a later version, in which the effects he studied before the motif were further refined.[6]

Gustave Courbet,
Stream in the Forest
(detail).

Monet's experience paralleled that of his future Impressionist colleagues Renoir, Pissarro and Sisley, each of whom experienced the strong pull of Barbizon style in the mid-1860s. Renoir painted both sober portraits inspired by Realist genre scenes, such as *The Cabaret of Mother Anthony* (1866, National Museum, Stockholm), and large-scale nudes, such as *Diana the Huntress* (1867, National Gallery of Art, Washington, D.C.), both redolent of Courbet's subject matter and style. Pissarro, at the Salons of 1864, 1865, and 1866, exhibited riverbank landscapes in the tradition of Daubigny (Glasgow Art Gallery and Museum, Kelvingrove; National Gallery of Scotland, Edinburgh; The Art Institute of Chicago). In 1866 Sisley exhibited *A Street at Marlotte: Environs of Fontainebleau*, which recalls Corot in its massing of farm buildings and both Daubigny and Courbet in its sober palette (1866, Albright-Knox Art Gallery, Buffalo, N.Y.). Edgar Degas, at the same Salon, exhibited a large-scale depiction of a *Steeplechase* (Collection of Mr. and Mrs. Paul Mellon, Upperville, Va.). An amalgam of

Realist landscape and figure painting, Degas's ambitious composition nodded to Courbet's dramatic scenes of the hunt, as well as to the images of figures in the landscape painted by his mentor Édouard Manet. By the end of the 1860s, however, the young artists of the nascent Impressionist movement were advancing in uncharted directions, beyond the idiom of Barbizon painting. In 1869, working side by side at the fashionable boating place of La Grenouillère, Monet and Renoir began to paint works in which the optical experience of sunlight falling on the rippling water was recorded on canvas with a new vocabulary of brushstrokes, inspired by Courbet and Manet, but seeking to invent an altogether new pictorial language.

These paintings marked a turning point in the history of the Impressionist landscape, but they flow from the experiments that Monet had conducted in the middle years of the decade. His careful, deliberate technique, particularly evident in the handling of the alternating lights and shadows in his views of the river, recalls the thick brushstrokes he used to paint the Rue de la Bavolle at Honfleur. It seems, moreover, that Monet again intended to use these riverside paintings to develop other canvases in the studio. In late September 1869 he wrote to Bazille from a village near the Seine: 'I do have a dream, of a picture, the bathing place at La Grenouillère, for which I have made a few bad sketches, but it's only a dream. Renoir, who has just passed two months here, would also like to paint this picture.'[7]

A conventionally ambitious, large-scale Salon composition that derived from these studies never materialised; it seems likely, however, that Monet sent a more developed version of one of the *pochades*, as he called them, to the Salon of 1870, along with an interior. The jury rejected both paintings.[8] Renoir shrewdly ignored his new landscapes and exhibited at the same Salon two magnificent, but less innovative, figure paintings: a Courbet-like *Bather with a Griffon* (Museu de Arte de São Paulo Assis Chateaubriand), nearly life-size, and *Woman of Algiers* (National Gallery of Art, Washington, D.C.), manifestly inspired by Eugène Delacroix's Orientalist subjects. In the wake of Monet's exclusion from the Salon, both Daubigny (long a defender of the young painter) and Corot resigned from the Salon jury in protest. But in spite of his absence from the exhibition, much was made of Monet's position at the vanguard of painting. Arsène Houssaye wrote: 'The two real masters of this school which, instead of saying art for art's sake, says nature for nature's sake, are MM. Monet (not to be confused with Manet) and Renoir, two real masters, like Courbet of Ornans, through the brutal frankness of their brush.'[9]

Although his first attempt to exhibit one of his 'bad sketches' of La Grenouillère was rebuffed, Monet was to exhibit another such work in the second Impressionist exhibition, in 1876. By that time, he had already presented to the public the famously sketchy *Impression: Sunrise* (Musée Marmottan–Claude Monet, Paris), the lightly worked view of the port at Le Havre that gave the Impressionist movement its name. That picture was initially shown at the first exhibition of the newly founded Société Anonyme Coopérative d'Artistes-peintres, Sculpteurs, etc., held in the former studio of the photographer Nadar on a busy commercial street in Paris. It opened on 15 April 1874. Writing ten days later, the satirist Louis Le Roy presented the comments of two fictional visitors to the Salon:

— . . . What does that painting represent? Look in the catalogue.

— *Impression, Sunrise.*

— *Impression*, I was sure of it. I said to myself, too, because I am impressed, there must be some impression in it. . . And what freedom, what easiness in the facture! An embryonic wallpaper is still more finished than that seascape there![10]

Le Roy's humorous exchange aside, the critics' response to the newly named Impressionists was generally favourable, and on the whole they praised the Impressionists' desire to exhibit free from the strictures of the Salon system.[11] Recognising that the group assembled artists from a wide variety of backgrounds, critics such as Armand Silvestre made an attempt to understand the painters' common motivations and to help his readers distinguish one participant from another:

At their head are three artists whom I have spoken of several times and who have, at least, the merit of being immutable in their goals. This immutability even touches on an aspect common to all three, which gives priority above all to the processes of their painting. At first glance, one is hard pressed to distinguish what differentiates the paintings of M. Monet from those of M. Sisley and the manner of the latter from that of M. Pissarro. A bit of study will soon teach you that M. Monet is the most able and the most daring, M. Sisley is the most harmonious and timid, M. Pissarro is, in the end, the inventor of this painting, the most real and the most naive. . . . What is sure is that the vision of things that these three landscape painters affect does not resemble in the least that of any earlier master; that it has its plausible side, and that it affirms itself with a character of conviction that does not admit the possibility of disdain.[12]

By the mid-1870s, in spite of the critics' recognition of close affinities between them, each artist had evolved a mature vision of how landscape might be painted. Both Renoir and Monet had formulated a wholly individual manner of painting in the open air. Renoir's *Woman with a Parasol and Small Child on a Sunlit Hillside* (cat. no. 55), painted about 1876, shows his distinctive feathered brushstroke, with which he suggests both the sheer white fabric of the reclining woman's dress and the soft tufts of grass on which she reclines; sharp contrasts between the foreground shadows of deep emerald green and the background highlights of bright yellow and white convey the sense of brilliant sunshine. Monet's 1875 depiction of his wife Camille sewing in a garden while a child is playing at her feet (cat. no. 41) employs a characteristic flickering pattern of small daubed or curved brushstrokes. Here, dark greens and reds are juxtaposed with brighter, lighter versions of the same hues. This has the result of conveying the action of the light on the bed of dahlias and the grassy verge that make up the background of the picture, while the figures are set off from the vegetation by their blue and white clothing.

Pierre-Auguste Renoir,
Woman with a Parasol and Small Child on a Sunlit Hillside
(detail).

The overall effect of these treatments of the figure in landscape is a sense of freedom and improvisation, contrasting sharply with the more classically refined surfaces of such works as Degas's *Race Horses at Longchamp* (Museum of Fine Arts, Boston), probably begun about 1871 and reworked in the mid-1870s. Degas, who in the 1850s had painted pure landscapes in Italy and had used landscape backgrounds in his early history paintings, in the 1860s specialised in painting people in everyday scenes, mostly indoors – at home, in a café, or at the opera. He rarely turned to landscape at this period except as background for his racing pictures. Unlike Monet and Renoir, Degas painted such landscapes entirely in the studio, reproducing or adapting from his keen memory scenes that he had witnessed in the suburbs of Paris. The seemingly careless arrangement of horses in the open air was misleading, for Degas arranged and rearranged the elements of the picture more than once before settling on the final pattern of jockeys and mounts.

A middle ground between the sense of improvisation that Monet and Renoir cherished and the calculated strategies of Degas can be found in the paintings of Pissarro and Cézanne. Working together in the environs of Pontoise and nearby Auvers in the 1870s, these friends evolved a more geometrically structured response to the landscape. Like Cézanne, Pissarro, who in these years turned to themes taken from the lives of the agricultural workers in his district, often chose to order his paintings by introducing straight lines or geometrical shapes, as in his *Sunlight on the Road, Pontoise*, of 1874 (cat. no. 28). In the middle years of the decade, both artists, along with Sisley, adopted a lightened palette in which deeper shades of green and brown were softened by the admixture of whites and greys. And all three artists, particularly Cézanne, employed opaque, layered paint structures that together with their carefully shaped compositions confirm the studied processes by which these ordinary views were elaborated.

As the loosely affiliated artists explored different manners of depicting the landscape, each member of the group chose his sites and themes according to his particular temperament. On the whole, however, the artists shared a preference for motifs that veered away from the conspicuously picturesque, avoiding the hackneyed compositional formats that they scorned in the work of Salon painters. Thus, Monet painted an uneventful section of the road outside Vétheuil (cat. no. 42), Pissarro painted an equally uninspiring street in Pontoise on a dingy, snowy day (cat. no. 27), and Sisley, who might have chosen to paint a fountain in the park at Versailles, preferred to paint the pumping station at the Marly reservoir (cat. no. 36). By choosing subjects and points of view that seemed to contemporary audiences not only unimportant but somehow undignified, the Impressionists emphasised the distinction between their landscapes and those of the Barbizon School and its adherents at the Salon.

In line with their avoidance of conventional motifs, the Impressionists' compositions typically are free of apparent sentiment or evident meaning, especially when compared with the landscape paintings being shown at the Salon in the 1870s. For example, Chintreuil's *Peasants in a Field* (cat. no. 11), makes use of pyrotechnic cloud effects above the bowed heads of the harvesters praying in the field. This painting, exhibited at the Salon of 1870, romanticises and glorifies the fertile landscape of France and its traditional agrarian economy. The Impressionists tended to avoid such easily recognised interpretations: although Pissarro often returned to similar themes of rural labour, which Millet had made famous a generation earlier, his scenes of peasants or villagers in the fields are, by contrast with Chintreuil's dramatic vision, notably matter-of-fact (see cat. no. 29).

During the 1870s, the Impressionists concentrated on depicting places close to Paris, along the Seine or its tributaries downstream from the capital, in such towns as Argenteuil, Bougival, and Pontoise. In the 1880s Monet abandoned the villages along the river Seine frequented by Parisians, in favour of sites – some equally touristic, others more remote in character – on the coasts of France. Monet typically avoided the views that Boudin had painted at the height of the Second Empire in such works as *Fashionable Figures on the Beach* (cat. no. 23), which exploited the relationship between sea and sky; instead he turned to painting the sea in juxtaposition with the land.

Monet's works of the early 1880s attest to his love for the rough coasts of Normandy, where Delacroix, Courbet, and Millet had painted in the previous generation. There, at Pourville, Fécamp, and Étretat, Monet explored motifs that he had first treated in the late 1860s and early 1870s. His 1881 *Sea Coast at Trouville* (cat. no. 43) seems to equate the windswept form of a tree beside the sea with a watchful human presence, just as Millet had done in his 1866 *End of the Hamlet of Gruchy* (cat. no. 13), a depiction of his native village. Similarly, the *Fisherman's Cottage on the Cliffs at Varengeville*, of 1882 (cat. no. 44) resembles not only that village view, but also another by Millet showing a group of stone buildings perched on the sea, the 1872–74 *Priory at Vauville, Normandy* (cat. no. 14). Monet, like Millet, felt a profound connection to the Normandy landscape: 'The countryside is very beautiful and I am very sorry I did not come here earlier,' he wrote to his companion Alice Hoschedé from Pourville in February 1882. 'One could not be any closer to the sea than I am, on the shingle itself, and the waves beat at the foot of the house.'[13]

Jean-François Millet, *End of the Hamlet of Gruchy* (detail).

A group of these Normandy landscapes by Monet was presented at the Impressionist exhibition of 1882, where just under a third of Monet's paintings showed such cliffside views, sometimes stormy, sometimes sunny – among them the *Sea Coast at Trouville*. Although both Monet and Renoir remained largely unconcerned with its organisation, the exhibition of 1882 was heralded by critics as a great moment for the Impressionist landscape painters, who one by one had dropped out of the most recent group shows but had now returned to the fold.[14] However, not all the Impressionists shared Monet's passion for coastal scenery. At the same exhibition, Sisley presented *Overcast Day at Saint-Mammès* (cat. no. 37), named after the village on the Seine near Moret-sur-Loing, the town where he had settled in 1880; he was to make this humble landscape the subject of much of his painting for the rest of his life (see cat. nos. 36–38). And Renoir was represented by a group of paintings lent by his dealer Paul Durand-Ruel. These included not only a large group of figure paintings but also views taken along the Seine and his new views of Venice, which he had painted during a trip to Italy in the autumn of 1881.

Renoir's contact with the Mediterranean world was to have lasting consequences for his art and for the history of Impressionist landscape painting. In late January 1882, on his return from Italy, Renoir stopped to pay a visit to Paul Cézanne in Provence, and there he painted the sun-drenched rock cliffs of L'Estaque (see cat. no. 57), above the bay of Marseilles, cliffs that Cézanne himself had painted a few years earlier. For many years Cézanne had divided his time between the region around Paris and the land between Aix and the port of Marseilles, and by the 1880s he was spending more time in the warmer light of his native Provence. In 1883, inspired by Renoir's enthusiasm for the Mediterranean, Monet forsook the Atlantic coast and returned with Renoir to Italy; on that trip, Renoir painted his *Landscape on the Coast, near Menton* (cat. no. 58). Monet went back to the Riviera alone early in the following year and painted both in Bordighera, on the Italian coast, and on the Côte d'Azur, producing his own view of the Menton coastline.

In Italy and the South of France Monet found the warm golden light that had attracted artists there for centuries, a light that had clearly marked the work of a previous generation, most notably Corot (see cat. nos. 1–3) and his contemporaries, including Paul Huet (cat. no. 4). After several years, Monet again returned to the South, this time to Antibes, where in the spring of 1888 he painted yet another group of canvases.[15] 'I can see what I want to do quite clearly but I'm not there yet,' he wrote to Alice on 1 February. 'I've fourteen canvases under way, so you see how preoccupied I've become.' Three weeks later, the painter wrote of his frustrations: 'Everything's against me, it's unbearable and I'm so feverish and bad-tempered I feel quite ill . . . it's a miracle that I can work at all with all these worries, but I'm beginning to earn a reputation here as a ferocious and terrible person.'[16] *Cap d'Antibes, Mistral* (cat. no. 48), which shows the snow-capped Alps beyond the Bay of Antibes, reveals the energetic and even ferocious brushwork that Monet adopted during this trip to paint the most agitated motifs that he discovered on the Mediterranean coast.

It was in Antibes, too, that Monet was to refine his practice of painting a fixed motif under changing conditions of light at different times of day, a practice that he was to develop almost into a system over the next decade. Monet had often painted multiple views of a particularly interesting motif, and he had already presented to the public groups of paintings of related subjects. In 1876 he had painted twelve views in and around the Gare Saint-Lazare, six of which he exhibited at the third Impressionist exhibition, in 1877.[17] In 1882 closely related views of the Normandy coast had constituted a kind of series within the paintings that Durand-Ruel selected to represent Monet at the Impressionist exhibition. As the decade drew to a close, in the early spring of 1889, Monet painted a group of landscapes in the valley of the river Creuse in a remote region of central France. Setting up his easel high above the spot where two small rivers converged, he painted the valley in vivid sunlight and in the gloom of twilight. These, following the paintings of Antibes, were steps in the process toward Monet's fully developed serial method, which he explored more deeply in the 1890s with such series as his 1890–91 *Grainstacks* (see cat. no. 49) and the 1897–98 *Mornings on the Seine* (see cat. no. 50), and in the first decade of the twentieth century with his triumphant series of *Water Lilies* of 1903–08, exhibited as a group in 1909.

In making these groups of paintings, Monet was also seeking out opportunities for independent solo exhibitions. He not only wished to be free of the constraints of the Salon but also hoped to create bodies of work that would set him apart from his former colleagues among the Impressionists. In 1886, once again, he was absent from the exhibition of the Impressionists. Like Renoir, he turned to Durand-Ruel, as well as to such galleries as Georges Petit and Boussod-Valadon, for exhibition opportunities. Durand-Ruel, for his part, sought to expand the market for the Impressionists beyond Paris, organising commercial exhibitions of their works in New York and Boston.[18]

'I am heartbroken to see all of my paintings leave for America,' Monet wrote to Durand-Ruel as early as 1888.[19] And although the Impressionists' works were received everywhere in the United States with the enthusiasm of at least a few collectors, they were always an easy target for satirists: 'The Impressionists have been exhibiting here in force lately,' wrote the critic of the Boston *Art Amateur* in May 1891:

> Curious paintings by young Bostonian disciples of Monet, or Manet, with unconventional, prismatic reddish hues for fields and trees, and streets and houses in pinks and yellows respectively, have appeared from time to time for a year or two. But these were ascribed to the enthusiasm and indiscretion of apostleship. . . But at last the news is circulated that leading Boston buyers of paintings – the first buyers, in other days of Millets, Corots, Diazes and Daubignys – are now sending to Paris for this sort of thing, and Impressionism becomes the fashion. Some of our leading landscape artists praise it and preach it; many of the younger painters practice it. . . . The old favorites, sticking to their own styles, take back seats, and one almost wonders if all the pictures of the past are going to be taken out into Copley Square and burned. Titian and Veronese and the old masters have faded, we are told; Rembrandt is brown; even Corot is stuffy, and as for Daubigny and the rest of the modern French school of landscape, they are virtually black-and-white. Courbet and [the Boston painter William Morris] Hunt couldn't see color in nature as it really is. Tone, so much prized and labored for in the past, must go; Motley and Monet are your only wear.[20]

Vincent van Gogh,
Houses at Auvers
(detail).

But the novelty of the Impressionists' style could not, of course, last forever. In the late 1880s Paul Gauguin (see cat. nos. 62 and 63), Georges Seurat, and Paul Signac (see cat. nos. 69 and 70), who had exhibited with the Impressionist circle, and Vincent van Gogh (see cat. nos. 65 and 66), whose brother Theo had sold Monet's works, rejected the Impressionists' methods, which they saw as overly dependent on optical effects, and searched for new stylistic means. Gauguin gradually abandoned the broken brushstrokes he had used in the early 1880s in favour of a new, radically simplified style. Seurat and Signac, likewise, left Impressionism behind to evolve a method of painting with small dots of colour, which a critic would term 'Neo-Impressionism.'[21] And Vincent van Gogh, who recognized Monet as the great master of contemporary landscape painting, nonetheless rejected the Impressionists' delicately nuanced palette in favour of an emphatically drawn, boldly coloured style, which he believed expressed his deep emotions.

Partly because of these challenges, Monet, Renoir, and Pissarro themselves altered their landscape styles in the final decade of the century. Monet evolved his famous series as a way of expressing his continuing belief in the power of visual sensation and in the validity of representing these sensations as a means of artistic statement (see cat. nos. 49 and 50). Renoir, who in the late 1880s had expressed his dissatisfaction with the modes of traditional Impressionism, in the 1890s approached a manner that associated his art with the great traditions of French painting, deliberately referencing such painters of the eighteenth century as Jean-Antoine Watteau and Jean-Honoré Fragonard. Thus, many of his late landscapes, peopled by beautiful young women (see cat. no. 60), seem like fictions, as he reduced 'the setting to little more than a freely brushed colored backdrop, with only the merest hints of natural features.'[22] Pissarro, who in the mid-1880s had briefly adopted the Neo-Impressionist style advocated by Seurat and his disciple Signac, returned to his structured compositions of the 1870s in such paintings as *Morning Sunlight on the Snow, Éragny-sur-Epte* (see cat. no. 30). At the end of the decade he embarked on a series of Parisian street scenes that seemed to bring his art back to the views of urban life that Monet, Renoir, and even Gustave Caillebotte had pioneered in the late 1860s and early 1870s. And, most remarkably, the figure painter Degas, who had once commented that 'if I were the government I would have a special brigade of gendarmes to keep an eye on artists who paint landscapes from nature,' took up landscape once again in the 1890s, even holding a solo exhibition of his imaginative landscape pastels in 1892.[23]

By the first years of the twentieth century, the artists of the Impressionist vanguard were internationally famous. Their paintings were shown in exhibitions and enthusiastically collected throughout Europe and North America, and a growing appreciation of their achievements was felt in Japan. The work of Cézanne, by contrast, had received little public recognition during his lifetime, except perhaps from a handful of critics and from other painters: it is interesting to note that Cézanne's *Pond* (cat. no. 34) was owned by the painter Caillebotte, while his *Turn in the Road* (cat. no. 35) passed from the collection of the critic Théodore Duret to the painter Paul-César Helleu and eventually to Cézanne's friend Monet. After the turn of the century, however, a young generation of painters – in which were counted Henri Matisse, Pierre Bonnard, Pablo Picasso, and Georges Braque – found in the works of Cézanne, as well as in the works of Gauguin and van Gogh, the inspiration for their vivid experiments with colour and radical distortion of form.

But the lessons of Monet and Renoir were not forgotten, for they had discovered, in their youth, a new direction for landscape painting. Respecting the genius of past art while breaking with its corrupted conventions, they sought throughout their lives to renew and reinvent their ways of seeing the natural world. Their art inspired not only their colleagues and contemporaries, but also generations after them: today, museum-goers and art lovers throughout the world cherish the enduring pleasures of the world that they find in the art of Monet and Renoir, delighting in the dazzling visual sensations that these painters brought to the Impressionist landscape.

Notes

1. Catalogue numbers in this and the following essay refer to the exhibition catalogue *Monet, Renoir and the Impressionist Landscape* by George T. M. Shackelford and Fronia E. Wissman, with contributions by Erika M. Swanson (National Gallery of Canada/Museum of Fine Arts, Boston, 2000), from which this essay is reprinted, by kind permission of the author.

2. Monet to the journalist Thiébault-Sisson, 1900, quoted in John Rewald, *The History of Impressionism*, 4th rev. ed.(New York, 1973), p.38.

3. Monet to Boudin, 3 June, 1859, quoted in Daniel Wildenstein, *Claude Monet: Biographie et catalogue raisonné*, (Lausanne, 1974), vol.1, p.419.

4. Monet to Boudin, 19 May, 1859, quoted in Richard Kendall ed. *Monet by Himself*, (London, 1989), p.18.

5. See John House, *Impressions of France: Monet, Renoir, Pissarro, and Their Rivals*, (Boston, 1995), p.178.

6. The painting, Wildenstein 1974, no.34, is in the collection of the Städtische Kunsthalle, Mannheim. See also House 1995, p.178.

7. Wildenstein 1974, vol.1, p.427.

8. See Gary Tinterow and Henri Loyrette, *Origins of Impressionism*, (New York, 1994), pp.436–38 (the rejected view of *La Grenouillère* is probably the one in Wildenstein 1974, no.136 [formerly Arnhold Collection, Berlin, presumed destroyed]), and Charles F. Stuckey, *Claude Monet, 1840-1926*, (Chicago, 1995), p.194.

9. Houssaye to Karl Bertrand, in 'Salon de 1870' in *L'Artiste*, (1870), p.319, quoted in Loyrette and Tinterow 1994, p.438.

10. Louis Le Roy, 'L'exposition des impressionnistes', *Le Charivari*, (25 April, 1874), pp.79–80, quoted in Berson 1996, vol.1, p.26.

11. For a critical review of the exhibition see Paul Hayes Tucker, 'The First Impressionist Exhibition in Context' in Charles S. Moffett et al. *The New Painting: Impressionism*, 1874-1886, (San Francisco, 1986), pp.93–117, especially pp.106–10.

12. Armand Silvestre, 'Chronique des beaux-arts: Physiologie du refusé – L'exposition des révoltés', *L'Opinion Nationale*, (22 April, 1874), pp.2–3, quoted in Ruth Berson, *The New Painting: Impressionism*, 1874-1886. Documentation, 2 vols. (San Francisco, 1996), vol.1, p.39.

13. Monet to Hoschedé, 15 February, 1882, quoted in Kendall 1989, p.100.

14. For an extended discussion of the seventh Impressionist exhibition of 1882, see Joel Isaacson, 'The Painters Called Impressionists' in Moffett et al. 1986, pp.373–93.

15. For a discussion of both of Monet's 1880s campaigns on the Riviera, see Joachim Pissarro, *Monet in the Mediterranean*, (Fort Worth, 1996).

16. Monet to Hoschedé, 1 February and 24 February, 1888, quoted in Kendall 1989, p.126.

17. See Juliet Wilson, *Manet, Monet, and the Gare Saint-Lazare*, (New Haven and London, 1998) for a discussion of Monet's paintings of the Gare Saint-Lazare in the context of Manet's work.

18. For a discussion of the early Impressionist exhibitions in the United States, see Hans Huth, 'Impressionism Comes to America', *Gazette des Beaux-Arts*, ser.6, vol.29 (April 1946) and Frances Weitzenhoffer, *The Havermeyers: Impressionism Comes to America*, (New York, 1986).

19. Monet to Durand-Ruel, 11 April, 1888, quoted in Wildenstein 1974, vol.3, p.234.

20. 'Art in Boston', *The Art Amateur*, vol.24, no.6 (May 1891), p.141, quoted in Eric M. Zafran, 'Monet in Boston' in *Monet and His Contemporaries. Masterpieces from the Museum of Fine Arts, Boston* (exhibition catalogue by Eric M. Zafran and Robert J. Boardingham, 1992, published in Japanese), p.37 (from the English-language manuscript in the Art of Europe paintings files at the Museum of Fine Arts, Boston.)

21. For a discussion of Neo-Impressionism, see Rewald 1978, pp.73–132.

22. John House in House et al. 1985, p.257.

23. Degas to Ambroise Vollard, quoted in Kendall 1987, p.308.

Paul Huet

French, 1803-69

Landscape in the South of France c.1838-39

Oil on paper mounted on panel, 35.6 x 51.7 cm

Fanny P. Mason Fund in Memory of Alice Thevin
(1987.257)

HUET PAINTED in the warmer climes of the South of France because of ill health. He was painting landscapes even before 1820 and was later strongly influenced by Constable. In its composition, this small oil sketch looks back to the ideal landscapes of seventeenth-century French masters, with the figures bathing in the foreground and the winding river receding to a mist-filled distance. The rapidity of its execution with its thinned-down, easy strokes and its clear light distinguish it from the finished works that Huet exhibited.

16

18

Constant Troyon
French, 1810-65
Fields outside Paris 1845-51
Oil on paperboard, 27 x 45.5 cm
The Henry C. and Martha B. Angell Collection
(19.117)

LIKE RENOIR, Troyon first trained as a porcelain painter and spent several years in the famous porcelain works at Sèvres. By the late 1830s, however, he was painting and exhibiting landscapes, and had begun to frequent the Forest of Fontainebleau. Troyon's choice of paperboard (compressed paper) as support indicates that he almost certainly made this small sketch on the spot, somewhere on the outskirts of Paris, since the material was more portable than a stretched canvas.

Théodore Rousseau

French, 1812–67

Gathering Wood in the Forest of Fontainebleau
c.1850-60

Oil on canvas, 54.7 x 65.3 cm

Bequest of Mrs. David P. Kimball (23.399)

TOGETHER, COROT and Rousseau are the acknowledged giants of the so-called generation of 1830. Rousseau worked for much of his career in the Forest of Fontainebleau, sixty-four kilometres southwest of Paris, where he lived close by his friend Millet. The landscape of the area became familiar to him; indeed, he successfully campaigned for Napoleon III to create the first artistic preserve in the forest in 1853. Assured that intruders could not destroy the great oaks, he painted them with great sympathy. Here, dramatically backlit by the setting sun, the old oak tree dominates the uncultivated landscape where peasant women gather faggots.

21

22

Antoine Chintreuil

French, 1814-73

Peasants in a Field or *Last Rays of Sun on a Field of Sainfoin* c.1870

Oil on canvas, 95.8 x 134 cm

Gift of Mrs. Charles G. Weld (22.78)

THE JULY 1873 issue of the *Gazette des Beaux-Arts* declared: 'M. Chintreuil loves to seize that which appears unseizeable ... the vegetable, geological, atmospheric complications attract him inevitably: ... when he succeeds he creates prodigies'. *Peasants in a Field* is one of those 'prodigies'. Chintreuil himself considered it one of his most important works and exhibited it at the Salon of 1870. A faithful follower of Corot, the artist knew the importance of creating an overall light effect and the striking yellow-orange sunset casts an encompassing golden glow on the field of harvested sainfoin (a perennial herb grown as fodder), creating an intense visual experience.

Jean-François Millet

French, 1814-75

End of the Hamlet of Gruchy 1866

Oil on canvas, 81.5 x 100.5 cm

Gift of Quincy Adams Shaw through
Quincy A. Shaw, Jr. and Mrs. Marian Shaw
Haughton (17.1508)

THIS PAINTING is a poignant homage to Millet's native village of Gruchy on the coast of Normandy. He has painted the stone house that stands at the end of the only street in Gruchy – beyond it the English Channel stretches to the horizon. So peaceful is the village, Millet tells us in a letter of 1868 to Théophile Silvestre that 'each act … here becomes an event'. And so the geese are making a bolt for the cottage door (their 'constant goal') and, in bright sunlight, a woman picks up a small child who is reaching out to the elm tree. Stark and misshapen from the buffeting winds, yet clinging to the coastal soil, the tree is a symbol of tenacity and strength.

26

Gustave Courbet
French, 1819-77
Stream in the Forest c.1862
Oil on canvas, 157 x 114 cm
Gift of Mrs. Samuel Parkman Oliver (55.982)

THIS LUSH, verdant landscape must have held immense appeal for Courbet's audience, people living in cities who wanted to be reminded of the invigorating qualities of secluded nature. The size and format of the canvas combined with the elevated viewing point (the spectator looks down on the stream) contribute to its impact. But, above all, it is the physicality of the paint-smeared surface that creates such a strong engagement with the spectator. Courbet frequently spread paint freely in long planes and ridges with a palette knife, as seen here in the tall, slender birch trees and the reflections in the water.

Johan Barthold Jongkind
Dutch, 1819-91
Harbour Scene in Holland 1868
Oil on canvas, 42 x 56 cm
Gift of Count Cecil Pecci-Blunt (61.1242)

ALTHOUGH LIVING and working in France, Jongkind made frequent trips to Holland. In the autumn of 1868, the year this view was painted, he was in both Rotterdam and Dordrecht, although this seems to be a generalised view of a harbour. Writing in 1872, Zola clarified the artist's working methods: 'It might be thought that he confides his subjects to the canvas in great haste, for fear of losing the first impression, but in reality he works on his paintings for a long time in order to achieve that utmost simplicity'. Monet always acknowledged his debt to Jongkind and the nascent Impressionists recognised in his works (and in those of Boudin) the point of departure for their own examination of light and atmosphere.

Eugène Boudin
French, 1824-98
Fashionable Figures on the Beach 1865
Oil on panel, 35.5 x 57.5 cm
Gift of Mr. and Mrs. John J. Wilson (1974.565)

Believing that 'everything painted on the spot always has a strength, a power, a vividness of touch that is not to be found again in the studio', Boudin was one of the major precursors of French Impressionism. He is best known for his paintings of the beach at Trouville with its fashionable holidaymakers, dating from 1862 onwards. His keen eye for bright coloured costumes and the crisp seaside air coincided with the growing taste for tourism among the French middle and upper classes. Although his palette is fresh and responsive to changes in light, Boudin never developed the broken touches of paint characteristic of the Impressionists.

31

Eugène Boudin
French, 1824-98
Figures on the Beach 1893
Oil on canvas, 36.5 x 59 cm
Bequest of William A. Coolidge (1993.32)

This strikingly minimal scene was painted towards the end of Boudin's career when his work became looser and sketchier. The figures – the tourists, the boys who fish and gather shellfish and the distant horse and cart – are reduced in significance compared to his earlier *Fashionable Figures on the Beach*. Instead, the formation and movement of the clouds, the motion of the water and the palette of black, blue and green capture the atmospheric effects of the rainstorm threatening on the horizon. Despite its sketchy execution, Boudin clearly considered this painting finished, for he signed and dated it.

Camille Pissarro
French (born in the Danish West Indies), 1830-1903
Pontoise, the Road to Gisors in Winter 1873
Oil on canvas, 59.8 x 73.8 cm
Bequest of John T. Spaulding (48.587)

P ISSARRO'S WINTRY scene of a street in
Pontoise, where he lived on and off for
twenty years, provided the artist with an
opportunity to focus on subtle colour
distinctions. The carefully modulated creams
and ochres of the buildings – very different
from the blue/grey tonality of Monet's
Entrance to the Village of Vétheuil in Winter
(cat. no. 42) – combined with the grey,
overcast sky, create the effect of a lightly tinted
sepia photograph.

Camille Pissarro

French (born in the Danish West Indies),
1830-1903
Sunlight on the Road, Pontoise 1874
Oil on canvas, 52.3 x 81.5 cm
Juliana Cheney Edwards Collection (25.114)

P ISSARRO SPENT many years in
Pontoise, a hillside town above
the Oise river and just forty-five
minutes by train from the Gare du
Nord in Paris. He invited his friends,
including Cézanne and Gauguin, to
join him, painting the rural/suburban
environment. A committed socialist,
Pissarro populated his Pontoise
landscapes with local inhabitants.
This casual scene takes place along a
road by the river, with the town
stretching along the far bank. Pissarro
and Cézanne often painted together
during the early 1870s, sharing
techniques and ideas. Here, the
harmonious, well-ordered
composition and descriptive
brushstrokes are reminiscent of
Cézanne's work.

Edgar Degas
French, 1834-1917
At the Races in the Countryside 1869
Oil on canvas, 36.5 x 55.9 cm
1931 Purchase Fund (26.790)

DEGAS HAS created a casual record of a day at the races at Argentan, a racecourse along the Normandy coast. In the foreground, off centre, he portrays the family of his friend Paul Valpinçon with their wet-nurse. With his choice of subject and a radically asymmetrical composition (suggesting his awareness of photography), Degas has demonstrated his intention of painting contemporary subjects, in a modern style. While the cropped carriage and horse suggest the artist's awareness of photography, the flattened composition with its minimal modelling points to the influence of Japanese *Ukiyo-e* prints, which Degas collected.

Paul Cézanne
French, 1839-1906
The Pond c.1877-79
Oil on canvas, 47 x 56.2 cm
Tompkins Collection (48.244)

I N T H E tradition of eighteenth-century
pastoral scenes, Cézanne presents a
disparate group of figures relaxing by the
side of a pond or river. Although somewhat
enigmatic, the subject-matter is secondary to
the artist's concern to depict volumes in
space. In the nineteenth century, this
painting was owned by Gustave Caillebotte,
a generous patron of younger artists and a
noted painter in his own right.

Paul Cézanne

French, 1839-1906

Turn in the Road 1882

Oil on canvas, 60.5 x 73.5 cm

Bequest of John T. Spaulding (48.525)

Monet once owned this landscape, one of the finest works from Cézanne's second period in Pontoise and Auvers. The theme of the winding road appeared in Cézanne's works as early as 1872. *Turn in the Road* shows an unpaved country road curving along the edge of a village, probably Valhermay, set in the hills between Auvers and Pontoise. The road cuts through the landscape, following the wall of the village houses, and then is suddenly lost from view at the first bend. The viewer's eye is thus invited to travel along the curve in the track, but at the same time is blocked from entering too far into the flattened space.

43

Alfred Sisley
British (worked in France), 1839-99
Waterworks at Marly 1876
Oil on canvas, 46.5 x 61.8 cm
Gift of Miss Olive Simes (45.662)

THE PARK of the Château de Marly was designed by Le Nôtre in the late seventeenth century as part of the great aquatic system that brought water from the Seine to the storage pools of the Château de Marly, eventually supplying the fountains of Versailles. Sisley has painted the waterworks, the so-called *machine de Marly*, that was rebuilt between 1855 and 1859, in pale, subtle tones. He used the architecture and the walkways to structure his composition. Their man-made order is softened by the screen of trees in yellows, greens and pinks, mirrored in the water with broken, horizontal strokes of colour.

Claude Monet

French, 1840-1926

Rue de la Bavolle, Honfleur c.1864

Oil on canvas, 55.9 x 61 cm

Bequest of John T. Spaulding (48.580)

ONFLEUR WAS a favourite site in
Normandy of the Barbizon painters and this
early painting by Monet serves to remind us that
the Impressionists' early sites were the very same
ones which the Barbizon painters had begun to
frequent in the 1840s and 1850s. By the 1860s,
towns like Honfleur were also very popular with
tourists and Monet painted there during his
summer trips to Normandy from Paris. The
muted colours and the solid angularity of the
buildings and shadows offer a marked contrast to
the more familiar Impressionist style of his later
works.

Claude Monet

French, 1840-1926

Camille Monet and a Child in the Artist's Garden in Argenteuil 1875

Oil on canvas, 55.3 x 64.7 cm

Anonymous Gift in Memory of Mr. and Mrs. Edwin S. Webster (1976.833)

Monet moved to Argenteuil, a small town along the Seine, in late December 1871 where he rented a large house with spacious grounds. He painted many views of the house and gardens, often including his first wife, Camille, and his son, Jean. These were a modern form of landscape, set in a secluded suburban garden, reflecting the trend for middle-class Parisians to move to the suburbs in the second half of the century. Despite this contemporary context, the iconography of a mother sewing, accompanied by her child, recalls Millet's earlier compositions.

Claude Monet

French, 1840-1926

Entrance to the Village of Vétheuil in Winter 1879

Oil on canvas, 60.6 x 81 cm

Gift of Julia C. Prendergast in Memory of her Brother, James Maurice Prendergast (21.7)

Vétheuil was a small, charming village on the river Seine, northwest of Paris. This wintry landscape shows the road to the railway station of Vétheuil, the village where Monet moved in 1878. The winter of 1879-80 was particularly severe. The transport system in the Ile de France region came to a halt and the Seine froze over. In Monet's picture, the snow is melting on the side of the road, revealing a confusion of blues, greens, ochre and red. The scenes he painted during the winter were the earliest works following the death of his first wife, Camille, in late summer, 1879.

Claude Monet

French, 1840-1926

Fisherman's Cottage on the Cliffs at Varengeville
1882

Oil on canvas, 60.5 x 81.5 cm

Bequest of Anna Perkins Rogers (21.1331)

MONET'S SEA views sold easily after the success of similar subjects at the seventh Impressionist group exhibition in March 1882. That summer, Monet was in the Dieppe area. He painted this stone cottage perched on the cliffs at Varengeville, just west of Dieppe, in full mid-day sun. The cottage, one of those cabins that had been built during the Napoleonic era as look-out posts, was probably used by fishermen for storage. The dense undergrowth – painted in lively flickering brushstrokes – makes it appear inaccessible, but its orange roof stands out brightly against the blues and greens of the sea and foliage.

54

Claude Monet

French, 1840-1926

Cap d'Antibes, Mistral 1888

Oil on canvas, 66 x 81.3 cm

Bequest of Arthur Tracy Cabot (45.542)

IN JANUARY 1888 Monet made his second trip to the Côte d'Azur, staying at the popular seaside resort of Antibes. During his four-month sojourn, he produced some thirty-nine paintings including three of the motif represented here: trees set against the sea and the 'chain of the Alps eternally covered with snow', as the artist described them. By repeating the subject under different weather conditions, and thus varying the colour tones and brushstrokes (here the long, loose strokes are suggestive of the effect of the mistral), Monet was progressing logically towards the series paintings of the 1890s.

Claude Monet

French, 1840-1926

Grainstack (Sunset) 1891

Oil on canvas, 73.3 x 92.6 cm

Juliana Cheney Edwards Collection (25.112)

GRAINSTACK (SUNSET) belongs to a series of at least twenty-five canvases that Monet painted of the motif in 1890-91. In May 1891, fifteen of them were shown together for the first time in Paris, to almost unanimous praise. The carefully constructed stack, which would have been fifteen or twenty feet high, dominates the landscape and is intersected at the centre by a line of farm buildings with thatched roofs. France in the late nineteenth century continued to regard itself as an agrarian nation, and the grainstack represents the prosperity of rural living. Painted at sunset, the image is aglow with hot, bright colours – hot oranges, red and burning yellow.

Claude Monet
French, 1840-1926
Morning on the Seine, near Giverny 1897
Oil on canvas, 81.4 x 92.7 cm
Gift of Mrs. W. Scott Fitz (11.1261)

IN 1883 Monet moved to Giverny, some sixty kilometres northwest of Paris, and in 1890 he bought a property there. The area around Giverny, and his own garden, provided the inspiration for series of paintings in the 1890s. This monochromatic riverscape is one of a series of pre-dawn views of the Seine at Giverny dating from 1896-97. Painting primarily with subtle strokes of carefully chosen blues, Monet used mauves and greens to deepen and complicate the picture's large rounded shapes, still indistinct in the early morning light.

Pierre-Auguste Renoir

French, 1841-1919

Woman with a Parasol and Small Child on a Sunlit Hillside 1874-76

Oil on canvas, 47 x 56.2 cm

Bequest of John T. Spaulding (48.593)

IN THIS painting, Renoir evokes a blissful scene of rural tranquillity. The luscious brushstrokes convey the humid heat of a summer day. The young mother, dressed in white, sinks into the tall grass, while the adventurous toddler investigates what is happening to the right, off canvas. Renoir merges his subjects into the same light as the background to suggest atmosphere and distance. All outline is blurred with the figures blending into the light soaked grass of the hillside. The woman's face is delicately painted, however, as is her collar.

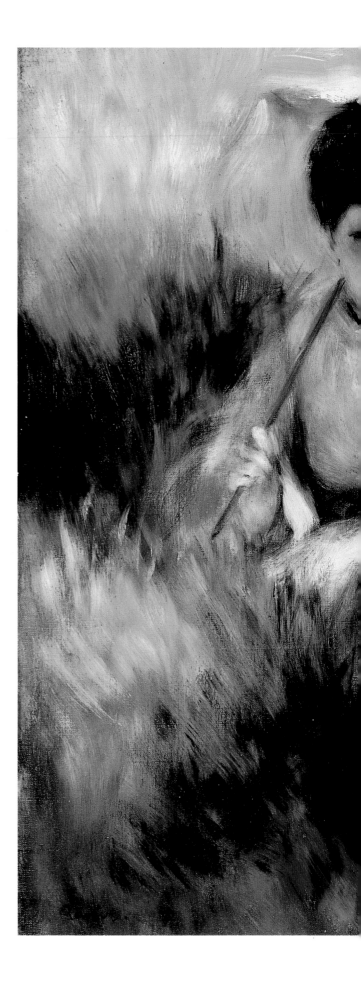

Pierre-Auguste Renoir
French, 1841-1919
Rocky Crags at L'Estaque 1882
Oil on canvas, 66.5 x 81 cm
Juliana Cheney Edwards Collection (39.678)

AT THE end of the 1870s, Renoir was becoming dissatisfied with the techniques of Impressionism. In early 1882, he worked alongside Cézanne at L'Estaque, west of Marseilles. 'I am in the process of learning a lot', he wrote to Mme Charpentier, 'while warming myself and observing a great deal, I shall, I believe, have acquired the simplicity and grandeur of the ancient painters'. There is a sense of structure and solidity in the ascent from the lower grassy slopes to the bolder forms of the rocks above in *Rocky Crags at L'Estaque*, due no doubt to the influence of Cézanne, as is the technique of small, parallel brushstrokes. But the scene is still suffused with sunshine and light.

Pierre-Auguste Renoir

French, 1841-1919

Girls Picking Flowers in a Meadow c.1890

Oil on canvas, 65 x 81 cm

Juliana Cheney Edwards Collection (39.675)

IN THE 1880s Renoir had already expressed his dissatisfaction with traditional Impressionism, and in his late landscapes sought to associate his art with the great eighteenth-century figures like Fragonard and Boucher. Here, in *Girls Picking Flowers in a Meadow* of c.1890, he reduces the landscape to an unspecific background, peopled with pretty young girls. The result is a softly painted vision of springtime, where Renoir has sought to link an image of modern life to the work of the old masters.

Paul Gauguin
French, 1848-1903
Entrance to the Village of Osny 1883
Oil on canvas, 60 x 72.6 cm
Bequest of John T. Spaulding (48.545)

IN 1883, Pissarro and his family lived in Osny, a village on the northwestern edge of Pontoise. Gauguin visited him there from mid-June until early July 1883. Pissarro kept this picture and, after his death, when his widow sold some canvases to Durand-Ruel, she identified it as by Gauguin. Gauguin was still an amateur artist at the time, working as a stockbroker with a bank in Paris, and was influenced by Pissarro's Impressionist method of broken brushwork. The composition – a road passing through a village with a mixture of thatched and tiled houses – is reminiscent of van Gogh's *Houses at Auvers* (cat. no. 66).

Paul Gauguin

French, 1848-1903

Forest Interior (Sous-Bois) 1884

Oil on canvas, 55.5 x 46.1 cm

Gift of Laurence K. and Lorna J. Marshall (64.2205)

P AINTED JUST one year later than his
Entrance to the Village of Osny (cat. no. 62),
this *Forest Interior* shows how noticeably
Gauguin's style has changed. His handling is
surer, the colour – greens, hot yellows and
oranges – more dramatic and the use of the
canvas to create a steeply rising, flattened space is
closer to Cézanne than to Pissarro. In 1884, the
year this was painted, Gauguin moved his family
to Rouen in the hope that the cost of living
would be less expensive.

Vincent van Gogh
Dutch, 1853-90
Houses at Auvers 1890
Oil on canvas, 75.5. x 61.8 cm
Bequest of John T. Spaulding (48.549)

IN MAY 1890, van Gogh left the South of France and settled in Auvers, close to Pontoise, where Pissarro, and Cézanne, had worked some years earlier. This view of the houses in the village is a bright, summer scene, concentrating on the red and green roofs and, above all, on the thatched roof of the house in the foreground. Van Gogh has varied his brushstrokes to distinguish between the thatch and tiles, stone and plaster of the buildings. In an unprecedented frenzy of activity, van Gogh painted about seventy paintings in the seventy days before he ended his life on 29 July 1890.

Paul Signac
French, 1863-1935
View of the Seine at Herblay late 1880s
Oil on canvas, 33.2 x 46.4 cm
Gift of Julia Appleton Bird (1980.367)

THE SMALL town of Herblay was just four stations beyond Argenteuil, along the line from Paris. Signac visited it in 1889 and this is one of a series of four pictures he painted of this view. In this example, the only recognisable feature of the town is the vertical form of the twelfth-century church tower. Signac used the Divisionist or Pointillist technique developed by Seurat – painting with deliberate strokes of pure colour – although here it is relatively freely applied. Sometimes he uses dots of colour, at other times oblong strokes, suggesting that perhaps this canvas was painted outdoors.

The Impressionist Landscape in the National Gallery of Ireland

FIONNUALA CROKE
HEAD OF EXHIBITIONS AND CURATOR OF FRENCH PAINTING
NATIONAL GALLERY OF IRELAND

ONE OF THE GREAT STRENGTHS of the National Gallery of Ireland's collection is its holding of French paintings of the nineteenth-century landscape. With this first exhibition to be shown in the Millennium Wing – *Monet, Renoir and the Impressionist Landscape* – we have, therefore, a magnificent complement to our own collection. This exhibition, which is drawn entirely from the Museum of Fine Arts, Boston, surveys the development of French landscape painting from Corot to the Post-Impressionists, that is, from the middle of the nineteenth century up to about 1910. Significantly, it also provides the first opportunity for the public to see a major collection of Impressionist paintings in Ireland. This Exhibition Guide highlights twenty-nine of the Boston paintings and directs the viewer to related works in the National Gallery of Ireland's own collection.

The core of the Gallery's collection came from Sir Alfred Chester Beatty who gifted ninety French nineteenth-century paintings to the nation in 1950. Over the following years, he gave an additional forty-eight paintings, two hundred and fifty-three drawings and miniatures, and six sculptures to the Gallery.

Born in 1875, Beatty had made his fortune mining in Northern Rhodesia. He was particularly attracted to Oriental and Near-Eastern art and went on to build one of the finest collections in the world. Today, this is housed in the Chester Beatty Library and Gallery of Oriental Art in Dublin.

Jules Breton,
The Gleaners
(detail).

Beatty accumulated his collection of paintings over half a century, although, unfortunately, we know little of his purchasing activity. He does not seem to have bought French paintings while he was living in New York prior to his move to Europe, although he had both ample opportunity and resources to begin a collection. (The Parisian dealer Paul Durand-Ruel had exhibited Impressionist works in Boston as early as 1883.) From our knowledge of those paintings for which we have some history, it is clear that he bought in both Paris and London, after he settled in London in 1912-13.

He concentrated on purchases of Barbizon School painters and their Realist contemporaries. Among the finest of these acquisitions was Jules Breton's *The Gleaners*, 1854 (NGI 4213) set against the backdrop of the artist's native village, Courrières. Breton was recording the time-honoured custom of gleaning the remnants of the wheat harvest, a back-breaking task but one in which he saw dignity and nobility in the toil of the labourers. Like Millet, Breton could paint these scenes from first-hand experience, but unlike the older painter, Breton generally censored the harsh realities of life from his paintings.

Beatty bought Troyon's *Valley of the Tocques*, 1855 (NGI 4282) in London in 1905. It is of about the same date as Boston's *Sheep and Shepherd in a Landscape* c.1854 (cat. no. 8), but is a larger, more finished work. Like Breton's *Gleaners*, Troyon's view of the Tocques valley near Honfleur in Normandy is an idealised image, celebrating French peasant life.

Despite the acquisition of some masterworks like *The Gleaners* and *Valley of the Tocques*, it may be said that Beatty tended to make modest purchases, often buying smaller works by the best-known artists – such as Jean-François Millet's *Country Scene with a Stile*, c.1872 (NGI 4265). Millet turned to pure landscapes only from the mid-1860s, late in his career, principally drawing on his native Normandy. The light-hearted focus on the geese – whose antics Millet recorded with nostalgia in letters to his friends – relates this work to *End of the Hamlet of Gruchy*, 1866 (cat. no. 13).

Jean-Baptise Corot had been painting pastoral scenes with dancing nymphs inspired by Claude Lorrain for over a quarter of a century (see his *Bacchanal at the Spring: Souvenir of Marly-le-Roi* of 1872, cat. no. 3). In his *Interior of a Barn*, 1874 (NGI 4218), however, painted when he was seventy-eight, he has chosen a more uncharacteristic subject. Strong sunlight enters the barn via the two windows and the door in the background and plays on the picture surface. With its palette of golden browns and yellows, this is a harmonious painting, the farmboy and dog blending into the overall treatment of sunlight on forms, reminding us that the picture dates to the year of the first Impressionist exhibition in Paris.

Jean Baptise Corot,
Interior of a Barn
(detail).

Beatty also included many of the lesser-known painters in his collection and in this regard he showed at most far-sightedness – the history of art is in many respects the history of artists who fall in and out of popularity – and at the very least, he proved that he acquired pictures that he liked, regardless of their author's fame. Very often, these works are of relatively small dimensions, and so of a comfortable size to fit in a corner of his home. He was not a connoisseur of French art. He sought advice before buying and he probably felt that he could not go too far wrong if he restricted his spending to small sums. 'You must not forget that I am not an expert on pictures', he said, 'I am quite good on Oriental Mss. but with pictures I depend a great deal on the advice of experts'.[1]

It was thought that because Impressionist works were not included in Beatty's gifts, that he excluded them from his purchases[2] and it is true that even works from his collection that are late in date were painted in a naturalist style. One may surmise that Beatty liked to see form, to recognise and understand the world as represented in his canvases. It may be that the modern subject-matter treated by the Impressionists and their break-down of traditional brushwork and light were less appealing to him – or perhaps just to his purse. He once commented to a journalist that he could buy ten decent French landscapes for the price of one Renoir![3]

Beatty's wife, however, was passionate about the work of the Impressionist and Post-Impressionist painters and, rather like the discerning Louisine Havemeyer, who persuaded her husband Henry Osborne Havemeyer into purchasing the French 'moderns' (most of their collection was bequeathed to the Metropolitan Museum of Art, New York), Edith Beatty gathered together a splendid collection of her own. Regrettably it was later sold to pay off death duties.

It is difficult to believe, however, that a man with Beatty's wide-ranging interests did not actually like the paintings of the Impressionists. In fact Boudin, Lépine, Forain and Raffaëlli (whose paintings were included in his gifts to the National Gallery of Ireland) had all exhibited with the Impressionists even if their names are not as familiar today as those of Monet and Renoir. And, after all, in 1928 he gave his wife £100,000 to buy Impressionist and Post-Impressionist works. It is likely that he indulged his wife's pleasure in collecting their paintings which he then left in her name. His comment to a journalist in 1965 declaring: 'Modern art? Can't understand it. Don't think there's a man born who can either'[4] surely refers to the more recent movements like the Cubists, the Expressionists, or Abstract Expressionism.

With the Chester Beatty gift, a rich array of Barbizon, Realist and Naturalist works was added to the collection of Impressionist pictures already held in the National Gallery of Ireland. Over the next three decades this was further augmented by a series of further gifts and astute purchases by successive Directors.

Notable among these was the Edward Martyn Bequest of 1924. This comprised a number of French nineteenth-century pictures and drawings, most of which Martyn had bought in Paris. Of particular interest in the present context is Claude Monet's riverscape, *Argenteuil Basin with a Single Sailboat*, 1874, (NGI 852). *Monet, Renoir and the Impressionist Landscape* contains two of Monet's paintings of Argenteuil: *Snow at Argenteuil* 1874 (cat. no. 40) and *Camille Monet and a Child in the Artist's Garden in Argenteuil* 1875 (cat. no. 41). The National Gallery of Ireland picture reminds us that this developing suburb, just fifteen minutes away from Paris by train, was unrivalled for its pleasure boating. The town itself is just glimpsed on the horizon, while the artist concentrates on capturing the refraction of light on the water.

Jean François Millet,
Country Scene with a Stile
(detail).

Alfred Sisley's *The Banks of the Canal du Loing at Saint-Mammès*, 1888 (NGI 966) was purchased in 1934. Of the Sisleys in the Boston exhibition, two depict scenes of Saint-Mammès, both earlier than 1888. All of these views feature, from varying viewpoints, the cluster of small houses which lies beside the locks at the mouth of the Canal.

Paul Signac's *Lady on the Terrace*, 1898 (NGI 4361) was purchased just twenty years ago, in 1982. Later than the artist's two works in the Boston exhibition, it is chromatically strikingly stronger. The earlier blues and yellows that we see in *View of the Seine at Herblay* (cat. no. 69) and *Port of Saint-Cast* (cat. no. 70) have here been replaced by tones of red, orange and violet. Mediterranean light entered his work when he went to Saint-Tropez in 1892, and as we can see in *Lady on the Terrace*, it gradually led him to transform his style towards a freer and less systematic divisionism.

The Museum of Fine Arts, Boston, has one of the most comprehensive collections of nineteenth-century French landscape painting. With *Monet, Renoir and the Impressionist Landscape* we have a wonderful opportunity to broaden our own presentation of the rise of this genre in nineteenth-century France. Following your visit to *Monet, Renoir and the Impressionist Landscape*, you will find the paintings discussed here in the Gallery's French Rooms in the Dargan Wing.

Notes

1. NGI archive, picture dossier 1527

2. Brian P. Kennedy, 'Sir Alfred Chester Beatty and the NGI', *Irish Arts Review*, vol.4, no.1, (Spring 1987), p.48.

3. *ibid.* p.44.

4. *ibid.* p.48.

Jules Breton

French, 1827-1906

The Gleaners 1854

Oil on canvas, 93 x 138 cm

Presented by Sir Alfred Chester Beatty, 1950

National Gallery of Ireland (4213)

BRETON CHOSE to situate *The Gleaners* on familiar ground, in his native Courrières (the village is depicted in the distance, its curious tapering church tower breaking the horizon line), and used his future wife, Elodie, to model for the standing female figure beside the small boy in the foreground. The subject was topical: the rights of gleaners were debated in the French Senate in 1854, and their rights were upheld in 1856. Breton's painting reminds the viewer of the structure of rural society, and that these families are the poorest in the village while the distant harvesters are employed workers.

Constant Troyon
French, 1810-65
Valley of the Tocques 1855
Oil on canvas, 100 x 149 cm
Presented by Sir Alfred Chester Beatty,
1950
National Gallery of Ireland (4282)

TROYON HAD already exhibited a painting of the Tocques valley in the official Salon exhibition of 1853. The critic of *L'Artiste* commented on it: '[the painting] reminds one of those lush Normandy pastures where the animals sink knee deep in thick, fresh grass. This scene exudes an abudance of life, a fresh slowing sap…'. Following this success, Troyon went on to paint several more views of the valley, celebrating French peasant life.

Jean-François Millet

French, 1814-75

Country Scene with a Stile c.1872

Oil on canvas, 54 x 64 cm

Presented by Sir Alfred Chester Beatty, 1950

National Gallery of Ireland (4265)

Although landscapes provided settings for his figure compositions, pure landscape only became important to Millet late in his career, from the mid-1860s. This idyllic view, which leads from the shady foreground through the gate to the gentle sunlit scenery beyond, has an unusually high horizon line. There is no human presence, just the rooftops of the farmhouse nestling on the slope of the hill, and the geese, scrambling to freedom through the twig barrier and leaving a trail of feathers in their wake.

Jean-Baptiste Corot
French, 1796-1875
Interior of a Barn 1874
Oil on canvas, 48 x 72 cm
Presented by Sir Alfred Chester Beatty, 1950
National Gallery of Ireland (4218)

COROT WAS trained in the classical tradition of landscape painting. Yet, through his innovations in landscape painting and his sensitivity to the effects of light, his work greatly influenced a younger generation of artists committed to realism. Although this interior of a barn was an unusual subject for him to treat, as a depiction of peasant life it is no less dream-like in its tranquillity and serenity than his idealised pastorals.

Claude Monet

French, 1840-1926

Argenteuil Basin with a Single Sailboat 1874

Oil on canvas, 55 x 65 cm

Edward Martyn Bequest, 1924

National Gallery of Ireland (852)

M ONET MOVED to Argenteuil in 1871. It was a picturesque, historic town and a developing suburb of Paris. In the second half of the nineteenth century, Argenteuil was unrivalled for Sunday trips and pleasure boating. Monet acquired a boat that he converted into a floating studio, and the river Seine and its sailing boats became the principal theme of his paintings. Light and its effect on the water's surface, however, is the true subject matter of this riverscape.

87

Alfred Sisley

British (worked in France) 1839-77799

The Banks of the Canal du Loing at Saint-Mammès, 1888

Oil on canvas, 38 x 55 cm

Purchased, 1934

National Gallery of Ireland (1966)

SAINT-MAMMÈS lies at the confluence of the Seine and the Loing river, and the Canal runs parallel to the Loing. Writing to Monet in 1888, Sisley described the region: 'It's not a bad part of the world, rather a chocolate-box landscape'. He painted a series of landscapes here, dating from 1883. Here, he has divided the canvas into horizontal bands of sky, the far bank with the red-roofed houses, and the foreground. His interest in surface texture led him to vary his brushstrokes – the expanse of sky is smooth, while the long reeds and foliage on the near bank are drawn in long criss-cross strokes.

Paul Signac

French, 1863-1935

Lady on the Terrace 1898

Oil on canvas, 73 x 92 cm

Purchased, 1982

National Gallery of Ireland (4361)

THIS IS the artist's wife, Berthe, on the terrace of their villa in Saint-Tropez. Using a startling palette of mauve, orange and green, Signac has created a harmonious and balanced composition, the figure deliberately blending with the landscape. He constructed this terrace so that he could enjoy the expansive view of the village and the gulf. The dabs of colour are quite loosely applied and follow the shape of the trees and the movement of the clouds.

Monet, Renoir and the Impressionist Landscape

Listed below, with their exhibition numbers, are the sixty-nine paintings from the Museum of Fine Arts, Boston, shown in the Millennium Wing of the National Gallery of Ireland from 22 January - 14 April 2002. For further information, see the exhibition catalogue, *Monet, Renoir and the Impressionist Landscape* by George T.M. Shackelford and Fronia E. Wissman with contributions by Erika M. Swanson (National Gallery of Canada/Museum of Fine Arts, Boston, 2000).

1. Jean-Baptiste Camille **Corot** (French, 1796-1875)
   Morning near Beauvais, about 1855-65
   Oil on canvas, 36.0 x 41.5 cm
   Juliana Cheney Edwards Collection 39.668

2. Jean-Baptiste Camille **Corot** (French, 1796-1875)
   Souvenir of a Meadow at Brunoy, about 1855-65
   Oil on canvas, 90.6 x 115.9 cm
   Gift of Augustus Hemenway in Memory of Louis and
   Amy Hemenway Cabot 16.1

3. Jean-Baptiste Camille **Corot** (French, 1796-1875)
   Bacchanal at the Spring: Souvenir of Marly-le-Roi, 1872
   Oil on canvas, 82.1 x 66.3cm
   Robert Dawson Evans Collection 17.3234

4. Paul **Huet** (French, 1803-69)
   Landscape in the South of France, about 1838-39
   Oil on panel, 35.6 x 51.7 cm
   Fanny P. Mason Fund in Memory of Alice Thevin 1987.257

5. Louis Gabriel Eugène **Isabey** (French, 1803-86)
   Harbour View, about 1850
   Oil on canvas, 33.3 x 47.9 cm
   The Henry C. and Martha B. Angell Collection 19.101

6. Narcisse-Virgile **Diaz de la Peña** (French, 1808-76)
   Bohemians Going to a Fête, about 1844
   Oil on canvas, 101.0 x 81.3 cm
   Bequest of Susan Cornelia Warren 03.600

7. Constant **Troyon** (French, 1810-65)
   Fields outside Paris, 1845-51
   Oil on paperboard, 27.0 x 45.5 cm
   The Henry C. and Martha B. Angell Collection 19.117

8. Constant **Troyon** (French, 1810-65)
   Sheep and Shepherd in a Landscape, about 1854
   Oil on canvas, 34.8 x 45.1 cm
   Bequest of Thomas Gold Appleton 84.276

9. Théodore **Rousseau** (French, 1812-67)
   Pool in the Forest, early 1850s
   Oil on canvas, 39.5 x 57.4 cm
   Robert Dawson Evans Collection 17.3241

10. Théodore **Rousseau** (French, 1812-67)
    Gathering Wood in the Forest of Fontainebleau,
    about 1850-60
    Oil on canvas, 54.7 x 65.3 cm
    Bequest of Mrs. David P. Kimball 23.399

11. Antoine **Chintreuil** (French, 1816-73)
    Peasants in a Field or Last Rays of the Sun on a Field of Sainfoin,
    about 1870
    Oil on canvas, 95.8 x 134.0 cm
    Gift of Mrs. Charles G. Weld 22.78

12. François-Louis **Français** (French, 1814-97)
    Sunset, 1878
    Oil on canvas, 47.1 x 56.3 cm
    Bequest of Ernest Wadsworth Longfellow 37.598

13. Jean-François **Millet** (French, 1814-75)
    End of the Hamlet of Gruchy (II), 1866
    Oil on canvas, 81.5 x 100.5 cm
    Gift of Quincy Adams Shaw through Quincy Adams Jr. and
    Mrs Marian Shaw Haughton 17.1508

14. Jean-François **Millet** (French, 1814-75)
    Priory at Vauville, Normandy, 1872-74
    Oil on canvas, 90.9 x 116.7 cm
    Gift of Quincy Adams Shaw through Quincy A. Shaw, Jr. and
    Mrs Marian Shaw Haughton 17.1532

15. Charles-François **Daubigny** (French, 1817-78)
    Road through the Forest, about 1865-70
    Oil on canvas, 64.5 x 92.5 cm
    Gift of Mrs. Samuel Dennis Warren 90.200

16. Charles-François **Daubigny** (French, 1817-78)
    Château-Gaillard at Sunset, about 1873(?)
    Oil on canvas, 38.1 x 68.5 cm
    Gift of Mrs. Josiah Bradlee 18.18

17. Gustave **Courbet** (French, 1819-77)
    Stream in the Forest, about 1862
    Oil on canvas, 157.0 x 114.0 cm
    Gift of Mrs. Samuel Parkman Oliver 55.982

18. Henri-Joseph **Harpignies** (French, 1819-1916)
Landscape with an Old Dam, 1882
Oil on paperboard mounted on panel, 40.0 x 33.4 cm
Juliana Cheney Edwards Collection 39.650

19. Henri-Joseph **Harpignies** (French, 1819-1916)
Evening at St-Privé, 1890
Oil on canvas, 73.7 x 54.5 cm
Bequest of Ernest Wadsworth Longfellow 23.486

20. Johan Barthold **Jongkind** (Dutch, 1819-91)
Harbour Scene in Holland, 1868
Oil on canvas, 42.0 x 56.0 cm
Gift of Count Cecil Pecci-Blunt 61.1242

21. Johan Barthold **Jongkind** (Dutch, 1819-91)
Harbour by Moonlight, 1871
Oil on canvas, 34.0 x 46.2 cm
The Henry C. and Martha B. Angell Collection 19.95

22. Louis Eugène **Boudin** (French, 1824-98)
Harbour at Honfleur, 1865
Oil on panel, 20.3 x 26.7 cm
Anonymous Gift 1971.425

23. Louis Eugène **Boudin** (French, 1824-98)
Fashionable Figures on the Beach, 1865
Oil on panel, 35.5 x 57.5 cm
Gift of Mr. and Mrs. John J. Wilson 1974.565

24. Louis Eugène **Boudin** (French, 1824-98)
Beach Scene: The Inlet at Berck (Pas-de-Calais), 1880
Oil on canvas, 54.5 x 75.0cm
Bequest of Mrs. Stephen S. Fitzgerald 64.1905

25. Louis Eugène **Boudin** (French, 1824-98)
Ships at Le Havre, 1887
Oil on panel, 35.0 x 26.5 cm
Gift of Miss Amelia Peabody 37.1212

26. Louis Eugène **Boudin** (French, 1824-98)
Figures on the Beach, 1893
Oil on canvas, 36.5 x 59 cm
Bequest of William A. Coolidge 1993.32

27. Camille **Pissarro** (French (b. Danish West Indies), 1830-1903)
Pontoise, the Road to Gisors in Winter, 1873
Oil on canvas, 59.8 x 73.8 cm
Bequest of John T. Spaulding 48.587

28. Camille **Pissarro** (French (b. Danish West Indies), 1830-1903)
Sunlight on the Road, Pontoise, 1874
Oil on canvas, 52.3 x 81.5 cm
Juliana Cheney Edwards Collection 25.114

29. Camille **Pissarro** (French (b. Danish West Indies), 1830-1903)
View from the Artist's Window, Eragny, 1885
Oil on canvas, 54.5 x 65.0 cm
Juliana Cheney Edwards Collection 25.115

30. Camille **Pissarro** (French (b. Danish West Indies, 1830-1903)
Morning Sunlight on the Snow, Eragny-sur-Epte, 1894-95
Oil on canvas, 82.3 x 61.5 cm
John Pickering Lyman Collection 19.1321

31. Antoine **Vollon** (French, 1833-1900)
Meadows and Low Hills
Oil on panel, 28.0 x 46.2 cm
Bequest of Ernest Wadsworth Longfellow 37.602

32. Hilaire-Germain Edgar **Degas** (French, 1834-1917)
At the Races in the Countryside, 1869
Oil on canvas, 36.5 x 55.9 cm
1931 Purchase Fund 26.790

33. Paul-Camille **Guigou** (French, 1834-71)
View of Triel, 1865
Oil on panel, 28.5 x 45.7 cm
Gift of Ananda K. Coomaraswamy 22.669

34. Paul **Cézanne** (French, 1839-1906)
The Pond, about 1877-79
Oil on canvas, 47.0 x 56.2 cm
Tompkins Collection 48.244

35. Paul **Cézanne** (French, 1839-1906)
Turn in the Road, 1879-82
Oil on canvas, 60.5 x 73.5 cm
Bequest of John T. Spaulding 48.525

36. Alfred **Sisley** (British (worked in France), 1839-99)
Waterworks at Marly, 1876
Oil on canvas, 46.5 x 61.8cm
Juliana Cheney Edwards Collection 45.662

37 Alfred **Sisley** (British (worked in France), 1839-99)
Overcast Day at Saint-Mammès, about 1880
Oil on canvas, 54.8 x 74.0cm
Juliana Cheney Edwards Collection 39.679

38. Alfred **Sisley** (British (worked in France), 1839-99)
La Croix-Blanche at Saint-Mammès, 1884
Oil on canvas, 65.3 x 92.3cm
Juliana Cheney Edwards Collection 39.680

39. Claude **Monet** (French, 1840-1926)
Rue de la Bavolle, Honfleur, about 1864
Oil on canvas, 55.9 x 61.0cm
Bequest of John T. Spaulding 48.580

40. Claude **Monet** (French, 1840-1926)
Snow at Argenteuil, about 1874
Oil on canvas, 54.6 x 73.8cm
Bequest of Anna Perkins Rogers 21.1329

41. Claude **Monet** (French, 1840-1926)
Camille Monet and a Child in the Artist's Garden in Argenteuil, 1875
Oil on canvas, 55.3 x 64.7cm
Anonymous Gift in Memory of Mr. and Mrs Edwin S. Webster 1976.833

42. Claude **Monet** (French, 1840-1926)
Entrance to the Village of Vétheuil in Winter, 1879
Oil on canvas, 60.6 x 81.0cm
Gift of Julia C. Prendergast in Memory of her Brother, James Maurice Prendergast 21.7

43. Claude **Monet** (French, 1840-1926)
Sea Coast at Trouville, 1881
Oil on canvas, 60.7 x 81.4cm
John Pickering Lyman Collection.
Gift of Miss Theodora Lyman 19.1314

44. Claude **Monet** (French, 1840-1926)
Fisherman's Cottage on the Cliffs at Varengeville, 1882
Oil on canvas, 60.5 x 81.5cm
Bequest of Anna Perkins Rogers 21.1331

45. Claude **Monet** (French, 1840-1926)
Road at La Cavée, Pourville, 1882
Oil on canvas, 60.4 x 81.5cm
Bequest of Mrs. Susan Mason Loring 24.1755

46. Claude **Monet** (French, 1840-1926)
Meadow with Haystacks near Giverny, 1885
Oil on canvas, 74.0 x 93.5cm
Bequest of Arthur Tracy Cabot 42.541

47. Claude **Monet** (French, 1840-1926)
Meadow at Giverny, late 1886 (?)
Oil on canvas, 92.0 x 81.5cm
Juliana Cheney Edwards Collection 39.670

48. Claude **Monet** (French, 1840-1926)
Cap d'Antibes, Mistral, 1888
Oil on canvas, 66.0 x 81.3cm
Bequest of Arthur Tracy Cabot 42.542

49. Claude **Monet** (French, 1840-1926)
Grainstack (Sunset), 1891
Oil on canvas, 111.4 x 130.2cm
Juliana Cheney Edwards Collection 25.112

50. Claude **Monet** (French, 1840-1926)
Morning on the Seine, near Giverny, 1897
Oil on canvas, 81.3 x 92.7cm
Gift of Mrs. W. Scott Fitz 11.1261

51. Claude **Monet** (French, s 1840-1926)
The Water Lily Pond (Japanese Bridge), 1900
Oil on canvas, 90.2 x 92.7cm
Gift of the Fuller Foundation in Memory of Governor Alvan T. Fuller 61.959

52. Stanislas Henri Jean Charles **Cazin** (French, 1841-1901)
Cottage in the Dunes
Oil on canvas, 46 x 55.5cm
William R. Wilson Donation 15.882

53. Stanislas Henri Jean Charles **Cazin** (French, 1841-1901)
Farm Beside an Old Road
Oil on canvas 65.1 x 81.6
Bequest of Anna Perkins Rogers 21.1330

54. Jean-Baptiste Armand **Guillaumin** (French, 1841-1927)
Bridge in the Mountains, 1898
Oil on canvas, 65.5 x 81.8
Bequest of John T. Spaulding 48.560

55. Pierre-Auguste **Renoir** (French,1841-1919)
Woman with a Parasol and Small Child on a Sunlit Hillside, 1874-76
Oil on canvas, 47.0 x 56.2cm
Bequest of John T. Spaulding 48.593

56. Pierre-Auguste **Renoir** (French,1841-1919)
Rocky Crags at L'Estaque, 1882
Oil on canvas, 66.5 x 81.0cm
Juliana Cheney Edwards Collection 39.678

57. Pierre-Auguste **Renoir** (French,1841-1919)
Landscape on the Coast, near Menton, 1883
Oil on canvas, 65.8 x 81.3cm
Bequest of John T. Spaulding 48.596

58. Pierre-Auguste **Renoir** (French,1841-1919)
Children on the Seashore, Guernsey, about 1883
Oil on canvas 91.5 x 66.5cm
Bequest of John T. Spaulding 48.594

59. Pierre-Auguste **Renoir** (French,1841-1919)
Girls Picking Flowers in a Meadow, about 1890
Oil on canvas, 65.0 x 81.0cm
Juliana Cheney Edwards Collection 39.675

60. Léon Augustin **Lhermitte**, (French, 1844-1925)
    Wheatfield (Noonday Rest)
    Oil on canvas, 53.2 x 77.5cm
    Bequest of Julia C. Prendergast in Memory of her Brother,
    James M.Prendergast 44.38

61. Paul **Gauguin** (French, 1848-1903)
    Entrance to the Village of Osny, 1882-83
    Oil on canvas, 60.0 x 72.6cm
    Bequest of John T. Spaulding 48.545

62. Paul **Gauguin** (French, 1848-1903)
    Forest Interior (Sous Bois), 1884
    Oil on canvas, 55.5 x 46.1cm
    Gift of Laurence and Lana J. Marshall 64.2205

63. Pascal Adolphe Jean **Dagnan-Bouveret** (French, 1852-1929)
    Willows by a Stream, 1908
    Oil on canvas, 65.4 x 81.4cm
    Gift of Robert Jordan
    from the Collection of Eben D. Jordan 24.216

64. Vincent **van Gogh** (Dutch (worked in France), 1853-90)
    Enclosed Field with Ploughman, 1889
    Oil on canvas, 53.93 x 64.51cm
    Bequest of William A. Coolidge 1993.37

65. Vincent **van Gogh**
    (Dutch (worked in France), 1853-90)
    Houses at Auvers, 1890
    Oil on canvas, 75.5 x 61.8cm
    Bequest of John T. Spaulding 48.549

66. Maxime Emile Louis **Maufra** (French, 1861-1918)
    Departure of Fishing Boats, Yport, 1900
    Oil on canvas, 54.1 x 65.2cm
    John Pickering Lyman Collection 19.1316

67. Henri Eugène **Le Sidaner** (French, 1862-1939)
    Grand Trianon, about 1905
    Oil on canvas, 70.5 x 94.5cm
    Bequest of Katherine Dexter McCormick 68.567

68. Paul **Signac** (French, 1863-1935)
    View of the Seine at Herblay, late 1880s
    Oil on canvas, 33.3 x 46.4
    Gift of Julia Appleton Bird 1980.367

69. Paul **Signac** (French, 1863-1935)
    Port of Saint-Cast, 1890
    Oil on canvas 66.04 x 82.55
    Gift of William A. Coolidge 1991.584

Index

Index of paintings in the exhibition illustrated in this Exhibition Guide, and of related works in the National Gallery of Ireland.

Millennium Wing

An acknowledgement to our Benefactors

Monet Renoir and the Impressionist Landscape is the first exhibition to be mounted in the Millennium Wing, with facilities purpose built to hold major international exhibitions. The National Gallery of Ireland is grateful for the support of its many benefactors, without whom the building would not have been possible. They include:

SILE DE VALERA TD, MINISTER OF THE DEPARTMENT FOR THE ARTS, HERITAGE, GAELTACHT AND THE ISLANDS
THE EUROPEAN COMMUNITY, EUROPEAN REGIONAL DEVELOPMENT FUND
GEORGE BERNARD SHAW

MARTIN AND CARMEL NAUGHTON
SIR ANTHONY AND LADY O'REILLY
LOCHLANN AND BRENDA QUINN

AIB GROUP
BANK OF IRELAND GROUP
ESB
FIRST ACTIVE PLC
LEWIS AND LORETTA GLUCKSMAN
GUINNESS UDV IRELAND
IRISH LIFE AND PERMANENT PLC
BRENDAN AND BERNARDINE MCDONALD

BRIAN AND EILEEN BURNS
CLANCOURT GROUP LTD
BRIAN AND ANNE DAVY
PV AND MARGARET DOYLE
MARY AND ALAN HOBART
HOWARD AND MERIEL KILROY
JOHN AND LEONORA KERRY KEANE
KAY AND FRED KREHBIEL
MARGERY AND ALASTAIR MCGUCKIAN
KEN AND BRENDA ROHAN
DON AND MARILYN KEOUGH
BRYAN AND ELISABETH MOYNE
ULSTER BANK

CRH PLC
GREEN PROPERTIES
EARL LINEHAN
THE FRIENDS OF THE MILLENNIUM WING
SIR DENNIS MAHON
NEIL MCCANN
A M O'MARA
WILLIAM REILLY
JOHN RONAN